THE COPING CAT
PARENT COMPANION

D1072270

Philip C. Kendall, Ph.D., ABPP

Jennifer L. Podell, M.A., &

Elizabeth A. Gosch, Ph.D., ABPP

Workbook Publishing offers evidence-based child and adolescent workbooks, treatment manuals, and training materials.

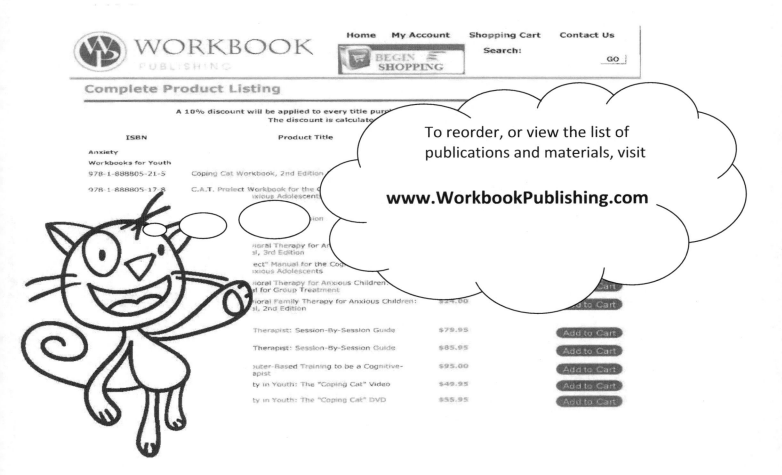

Available are

- DVDs for training in the provision of the intervention programs and treatments.
- An interactive computer-assisted program (*Camp Cope-A-Lot*) to address anxiety in youth.
- Materials for youth with depression, anger management issues, and impulsivity.
- Materials for *EMOTION*, a group program for both anxiety and depression, that has compatible materials for working with parents.
- Materials for anxiety in youth, including child anxiety (*Coping cat program*; *Brief Coping cat program*) and anxiety in adolescents (*C.A.T. Project*).

Philip C. Kendall, Ph.D., ABPP

Child and Adolescent Anxiety Disorders Clinic (CAADC)

Temple University

Jennifer L. Podell, M.A.

Child and Adolescent Anxiety Disorders Clinic (CAADC)

Temple University

Elizabeth A. Gosch, Ph.D., ABPP

Philadelphia College of Osteopathic Medicine

THE COPING CAT
PARENT COMPANION

COPYRIGHT © 2010
BY WORKBOOK PUBLISHING, INC.

ISBN: 978-1-888805-43-7

ILLUSTRATION BY ROBBI @ROBBIBEHR.COM

All rights reserved. None of the pages or materials may be reproduced by any means, stored in a retrieval system, or transmitted in any form or by any means, electronic, mechanical, photocopying, microfilming, recording, or otherwise, without the written permission from the copyright holders.

Printed in the United States of America

WORKBOOK PUBLISHING, INC.
P.O. BOX 67
ARDMORE, PA 19003-0067 USA
WWW.WORKBOOKPUBLISHING.COM

Table of Contents

Introduction to the Parent Companion

The Coping Cat Program

Introduction to the Parent Companion

I. Welcome to the *Coping Cat Program*

Hello and welcome to the *Coping Cat Program*. We designed this *Parent Companion* to help you understand the experiences your child will have as he or she completes the program. This *Parent Companion* provides you with information about anxiety, about its treatment, and about the ways you may be involved in your child's treatment.

Many children can learn to manage worry, anxiety, stress, and avoidance through our program. The goal of the program is not to eliminate all anxiety but rather to learn to identify, regulate, and cope with it more effectively. When children experience success in coping with anxiety-inducing experiences, their subsequent anxiety diminishes. We describe this as "turning down the volume" of the anxiety. Experiencing anxiety is normal, but when anxiety interferes with your child's life or causes him/her undue distress it becomes a problem.

The *Coping Cat Program* typically consists of approximately 16 sessions. Sessions are usually scheduled for one hour once per week. Although the majority of sessions take place between a therapist and your child, your participation and input is very important. In addition to "checking in" with your child's therapist each week, parents meet with the therapist alone for two sessions. These sessions provide additional time for you to discuss concerns, receive information, and plan ways to facilitate your child's progress. We find these parent sessions to be the most helpful when parents and important caretakers attend. Sometimes one parent is more involved in childcare than another; however, children benefit the most from the program when all parents/caregivers actively participate. In the first half of the program, your child will learn a variety of anxiety management strategies. In the second half, your child will practice applying the strategies that have been learned in real-world, anxiety-provoking situations.

The *Coping Cat Program* takes a cognitive-behavioral approach to helping children with anxiety problems, specifically children who experience symptoms consistent with generalized anxiety disorder, social phobia, and separation anxiety disorder. The overall goal is to teach children to recognize signs of anxious arousal and to implement strategies to better cope with the challenges in their lives. Children learn a 4-step plan, called the FEAR Plan, to organize the steps used to cope with anxiety. The children then apply the FEAR plan to the real situations that they associate with anxiety (e.g., taking tests, being away from a parent, talking to a peer). A key component of the *Coping Cat Program* is taking the time needed to practice applying anxiety management strategies in real, anxiety-provoking situations. Children start by applying the FEAR plan to low anxiety situations and then move to practicing in higher anxiety situations in a gradual progression that suits the child's needs.

What makes up the FEAR plan? Although the steps will be discovered by and explained to your child in more detail, a brief overview is worthwhile. In the first step, children learn to identify their anxious feelings and physical sensations associated with anxiety by asking themselves, "What am I **F**eeling?" and/or "Am I **F**eeling Frightened?". They use their own body cues to recognize when they are experiencing anxiety. Children then begin to identify the thoughts and beliefs that may contribute to their increasing anxious arousal by asking themselves, "What am I **E**xpecting to happen?" and/or "**E**xpecting bad things to happen?" Such thoughts are usually akin to being hurt or embarrassed. Children progress to challenging unhelpful thoughts (anxious self-talk) and using more helpful, coping self-talk. Children engage in problem solving and alternative ways of handling anxiety-provoking situations. They prompt themselves to engage in these activities by asking, "What **A**ttitudes and Actions will help?". After making a plan, they implement the fourth step, "**R**esults and Rewards." In this step, children realistically evaluate their coping efforts and are rewarded for their efforts to cope with their anxiety. Rewards are not based on judgments, but on effort. The steps spell "FEAR," and children use the FEAR plan as part of their personal anxiety management strategies in real situations.

You and your child will learn more about anxiety and ways to cope with it as you progress through the program. Some strategies may work better for you and your child than others. We know from past experience that the strategies work best when individually tailored to you and to your child. That's why we think of our program as a team approach. Your therapist is an expert in helping kids with anxiety, but the program works best when everyone collaborates. Some children demonstrate quick and favorable benefits from the program, but most gradually improve as they learn the anxiety management strategies and apply them to real world situations. Please feel free to talk with your child's therapist about any questions or concerns as your child moves through the *Coping Cat Program*.

II. What is anxiety and where might it come from?

- Anxiety is an evolutionary and adaptive response. We all need a certain level of anxiety in order to be alert and function effectively. If we didn't have any anxiety we might not be cautious when caution is warranted. Anxiety can even enhance our performance at times. Being a little nervous about a test may motivate us to study harder, and being nervous before a game may help us to perform better. Mild anxiety can even serve a thrill-seeking function. This might explain why certain people like roller-coasters or watching scary movies because it makes them a little anxious. Too much anxiety, however, can cause a great deal of distress. It gets in the way of school and work as well as relationships with friends and family.

- Where does anxiety come from? Our bodies have an automatic response to danger known as the "fight or flight" response. This response has physiological, psychological, and emotional aspects. When we sense danger our nervous system becomes activated: adrenaline is released into the body, the heart beats faster, breathing rate increases, thinking becomes rapid, and fear develops. Once the danger passes, our bodies and minds return to their resting state.

- We all have an internal alarm that is activated by danger. For children with anxiety this alarm can be viewed as overly sensitive, and it activates the "fight or flight response" too often and too quickly. The alarm signals to the body that there is danger when in reality there is not. For children with anxiety, the world appears to be a dangerous place. They live in a constant state of worry, which often times is accompanied by physical symptoms such as headaches and stomachaches. Other physical red flags of anxiety include trouble breathing, complaints of nausea, sweating, feeling dizzy, faint, or light headed, heart racing or beating faster than normal, and shaking or feeling jittery.

- Anxiety/worry can take many forms. These are some of the ways that parents have described their children….

  - ❖ "He worries all the time…about anything and everything"

  - ❖ "She can't handle change"

  - ❖ "He's too afraid to try anything new"

  - ❖ "She's like my shadow…following me around the house wherever I go"

  - ❖ "He won't go over to a friend's house"

  - ❖ "She gets so worked up she can't sleep"

  - ❖ "He has a stomachache all the time"

- Think about why you brought your child in for treatment. Do any of these statements sound familiar? On the following page is a list of the three most common anxiety disorders that are treated by the *Coping Cat Program*. Many kids have characteristics that cut across the categories listed below. These categories are one way to organize and describe different anxiety disorders. You may be asking yourself what makes something a disorder. "I know that my child worries but does he/she really have a disorder?" Worry/anxiety is classified as a disorder when there is extreme distress and impairment. Chances are your child's anxiety is interfering with his/her daily life and causing a great deal of distress.

- After you and your child completed the diagnostic interview, your child may have received one or more of the following diagnoses:

  - ❖ *Generalized Anxiety Disorder* (GAD). GAD is characterized by excessive worry and anxiety over a variety of things including: grades, performance in sports/art/music, punctuality, family issues, natural disasters, and health. A child with GAD cannot control his/her worry and this worry interferes with daily life. GAD includes a number of physical symptoms such as restlessness, fatigue, an inability to sleep, difficulty concentrating, irritability and muscle tension. Children with GAD tend to be very critical of themselves and they may strive for perfection. They may also seek constant approval and reassurance from others.

  - ❖ *Separation Anxiety Disorder* (SAD). SAD is characterized by developmentally inappropriate and excessive anxiety upon separation from a loved one or

caregiver. This separation causes significant distress or impairment in the child's academic, social, or other general functioning. A child with SAD might worry that something bad is going to happen to the caregiver or themselves when separated. Many children with SAD try to avoid going places by themselves, refuse to go to camp or school, are reluctant to go on sleepovers, follow their parents around the house, and a few may have nightmares about being separated from their parents.

- ❖ *Social Phobia* (SP). SP is an excessive fear of one or more social or performance situations. The most commonly feared situations include performing in front of others, joining or starting a conversation, speaking in class, and being the center of attention. Children with social phobia often avoid social activities, and this leads to impairments at school as well as with social relationships. Social phobia usually peaks during adolescence when social relationships are the most crucial. Signs of social phobia include avoidance of eye contact, speaking softly or mumbling, avoidance of ordering food in restaurants, minimal contact with peers, being overly concerned with negative evaluation, difficulty with public speaking, difficulty reading aloud, or fear of being called on in class. When a child with social phobia is in an anxiety-provoking situation he/she may exhibit physical symptoms such as sweating, racing heart, stomachaches, dizziness, crying, tantrums, and freezing.

- Regardless of the content of the worry, it becomes maladaptive when it is excessive, uncontrollable, and when it interferes with the child's functioning. When thinking about anxiety it is important to keep in mind that fear and anxiety are a natural part of human life at every age and every developmental stage. However, certain fears and worries seem to be more common during certain stages of youth. In the early years, children tend to be afraid of loud noises, strangers, the dark, certain animals, or imaginary things likes ghosts and monsters. Fears about physical danger and separating from loved ones are also common. In adolescence concerns about social situations and being embarrassed are prominent. These fears and worries can become a disorder when the worry is not developmentally appropriate, when it causes significant distress and interference, and when it has been going on for at least 6 months.

- Anxiety is one of the most common disorders in childhood and without treatment can have a number of negative consequences including substance abuse, depression, and anxiety in adulthood.

III. Treatment for anxiety in youth

- Although severe anxiety is highly impairing, the good news is that there are treatments available. Most children can overcome their fears by gradually facing them. Each time your child faces and copes with a feared situation it becomes less frightening.

- In the *Coping Cat Program* your child will learn how to cope with his* anxiety. This program uses a type of therapy known as cognitive-behavioral therapy (CBT). CBT addresses how we think (cognition), how we feel (emotion), and how we act (behavior), and recognizes that they interact. In CBT we focus on how our thoughts about a situation can determine our emotional reactions.

- The idea that how we think influences how we feel plays an important role in the treatment of anxiety. In addition, how we act in a situation depends on the consequences that follow our behavior. For example, if something good follows a behavior we are more likely to continue doing that behavior. On the other hand if something unfavorable happens following a behavior that behavior is likely to decrease or even stop.

- As we look at the role of thoughts, feelings, and behaviors we see how each can contribute to the development and/or maintenance of anxiety. Let's look at a child who has a fear of raising his hand in class. He thinks that if he raises his hand and does not know the answer to a question, his classmates will laugh at him. With this thought, the child never raises his hand in class. When he goes to class he fears being called on and this leads him to continue not to raise his hand. We can see here how a cycle of avoidance is created and how anxiety can spiral.

- The three main aspects of anxiety that we focus on are (1) physical and emotional reactions (feelings), (2) negative thoughts (cognitions), and (3) avoidance of feared situations (behaviors).

- The *Coping Cat Program* has two parts. The first part focuses on helping your child learn to identify when he is feeling anxious as well as introducing him to strategies to manage or reduce anxiety. These strategies are presented as a set of steps known as the "FEAR" plan that your child may carry with him and draw from when he is feeling anxious.

- You too will learn all about the FEAR plan throughout this *Parent Companion*. The strategies your child will learn include: identifying bodily arousal, engaging in relaxation, recognizing anxious thoughts, and problem-solving. These skills are taught in a sequence that allows your child to build skill upon skill.

---

* For ease in reading this Parent Companion we refer to the therapist as "she" and the child as "he" throughout the remaining pages

- The second part of the program focuses on exposure tasks--exposing your child to anxiety-provoking situations while he gets to use and practice the skills he learned. The goal of this program is to teach your child to recognize signs of anxiety and use these signs as cues to use anxiety management strategies. Coping skills do not cure anxiety—rather, they provide your child with tools to face stressful situations more courageously.

- You may be asking yourself what you can do to help your child during this program. Throughout this *Parent Companion* you will read about what your child is learning in each session, and you will be provided with tips on what you can do to facilitate your child's learning. In general, we suggest that you be sensitive, provide positive feedback for effort, be consistent, seek additional resources when needed, and be open to collaborating with your child's therapist. Try not to make adjustments in your life and your child's life to avoid anxiety-provoking situations (i.e., do not drive your child to school everyday because he is afraid to ride the bus). As a parent it is important to encourage your child to be brave. If you have questions about how to do this ask your child's therapist for suggestions.

The *Coping Cat Program*

IV. Getting to know each other

- During the first session your child and his therapist will spend time getting to know each other. Children may be nervous during the first session. It can feel strange coming to a new setting and sharing your fears and worries with a new person! Therapists are trained individuals who have experience working with children with anxiety. It can take some time for your child to warm up to a therapist, and it is natural for your child to be hesitant at first about coming to therapy. We have found that most kids end up liking therapy.

- Your child will learn to identify when he is feeling anxious, recognize anxious thoughts, and use appropriate coping strategies. During the first few sessions your child will simply learn some of the basics about anxiety. As we have discussed, anxiety is a normal reaction, and anxiety problems are very common in children. It is important for your child to know that he is not strange or weird or different because he worries. In fact, chances are there are other children at your child's school or in your neighborhood who also experience anxiety. During the first few sessions your child and his therapist will spend time figuring out how to recognize when your child is anxious. Fun and play are emphasized during therapy sessions.

- An important part of the program is active participation both in and out of session. Your child will be assigned "take home" work known as a "Show That I Can Task" (STIC) task. These are tasks that the child will complete and record in his Coping Cat workbook. Your child will earn points/stickers for completing his STIC tasks, and these can be exchanged for small prizes/rewards. Rewards provide children with motivation to continue trying new things.

V. Identifying anxious feelings

- In this session your child and therapist work on identifying a variety of different feelings. The goal of this session is to help your child distinguish anxious or worried feelings from other feelings. The therapist discusses the idea that different facial expressions can serve as clues to people's feelings. For example, someone who is smiling is likely to be feeling happy while someone whose eyebrows are raised and mouth is wide open might be feeling surprised or nervous.

- In addition, people's bodies can do different things in response to different feelings. Your child and his therapist will spend some time talking about feelings and their corresponding physical reactions and expressions. For example, someone who is sad may have a frown on their face and be crying, while someone who is nervous may be sweating and shaking.

- Your child and therapist will work to identify your child's own somatic responses to anxiety. Once the child understands that different feelings correspond to different expressions, the therapist works with the child to normalize his own experience of fears and anxiety.

VI. *What's that your body is saying?*

- Your child and therapist review anxious feelings, somatic cues, and work to identify your child's specific somatic responses. We all feel a variety of physical responses to anxiety. These can include sweating, shaking, racing heart, butterflies in the stomach, headaches, difficulty speaking, and/or muscle tension. Some children are very good at identifying the cues their bodies send them when they are feeling nervous. An important part of this program is "tuning in" to the cues your body is sending you.

- Your child is introduced to the first step in the "FEAR" plan. The first step in managing anxiety is checking in with your body and asking, **"am I feeling frightened?"** Your child is taught to identify the clues that his body is sending him. For example, the child who is afraid to raise his hand in class might come to know that he is nervous because he gets a stomachache before school, his heart starts to race when other kids raise their hands, or he notices that his hands gets sweaty. Once you can recognize that you are feeling nervous you can take action.

- When people are nervous they may feel some physical symptoms including stomachaches, headaches, and dizziness. Some children with anxiety go to the school nurse or leave school early because they report feeling sick. It is often difficult to figure out if your child is sick or feeling anxious. If your child has a fever, is vomiting, or showing other signs of an illness it is a good idea to keep him home from school. In some cases (you can review these with your child's therapist and/or physician) your child may be feeling ill because he has to face an anxiety-provoking situation (e.g., a test at school the next day). In these situations it is best to help your child go to school even though he is feeling uncomfortable physical symptoms. If your child stays home when he feels these physical symptoms he learns that he can avoid facing his fears because he is "sick." Figuring out when these symptoms are due to an illness and when they are due to anxiety can be very difficult, but the benefits make it worthwhile. You and your child can work with the therapist to help figure this out.

VII. *Learning to relax*

- One of the first strategies your child will learn to manage his anxiety is learning to relax the body. Using the "F" step of the FEAR plan your child has learned to identify the signals that his/her body sends when he is feeling nervous. These signals (e.g., racing heart, sweating, etc.) can be associated with tension. Tension can be reduced by relaxation.

- There are a variety of techniques that can be used to help relax. In the *Coping Cat Program* we use deep breathing and progressive muscle relaxation. Your child and therapist will practice relaxing in session and you may be invited to join. Together you may complete a series of exercises that will teach your child how relaxed muscles feel compared to tight ones.

- Once your child understands how to help himself become more relaxed, the therapist and child will work together to identify when relaxation may be useful. For example, it is unlikely that the child can engage in full progressive muscle relaxation each time he is

feeling anxious. However, the child may recognize that taking a few breaths and relaxing certain muscle groups might be useful.

- Practicing relaxing may feel strange at first but the more you do practice the more natural it will become. If your child learns how to relax his body when anxious feelings and sensations start, he will be much better prepared to manage anxiety.

- As a parent you can help your child learn be an expert at relaxing. Allow your child to teach you the relaxation strategies he learned in session. Don't tell him to "relax" but let your child show *you* how to relax. Practicing relaxing when you are not anxious is as important as practicing when you are anxious. At the end of this session your child will be given a relaxation CD to take home and listen to. Below is the relaxation script used in this CD.

Relaxation script for grades K-4 (developed by Koeppen, 1974)[1]

To begin the relaxation session, have the child sit in a comfortable chair and close their eyes. Soft, slow music can be playing in the background. When reading the script, speak in a soft, even tone. Pause between sentences.

HANDS AND ARMS: "Pretend you have a whole lemon in your left hand. Now squeeze all the juice out. Feel the tightness in your hand and arm as you squeeze. Now drop the lemon. Notice how your muscles feel when they are relaxed. Take another lemon and squeeze it. Try to squeeze. Try to squeeze it harder than you did the first one. That's right. Real hard. Now drop your lemon and relax. See how much better your hand and arm feel when they are relaxed. Once again, take a lemon in your left hand and squeeze all the juice out. Don't leave a single drop. Squeeze hard. Now relax and let the lemon fall from your hand." (*repeat this process with the right hand and arm.*)

ARMS AND SHOULDERS: "Pretend you are a furry, lazy cat. You want to stretch. Stretch your arms out in front of you. Place them up high over your head, way back. Feel the pull in your shoulders. Stretch higher. Now just let your arms drop back to your side. Okay, kittens, let's stretch again. Stretch your arms out in front of you. Raise them over your head. Put them back, way back. Pull hard."

"Now let them drop quickly. This time let's have a great big stretch. Try to touch the ceiling. Stretch your arms way out in front of you. Raise them way up high over your head. Push them way, way back. Notice the tension and pull in your arms and shoulders. Hold tight now. Great. Let them drop very quickly and feel how good it is to be relaxed. It feels good and warm and lazy."

[1]The following script is taken from Koeppen, A.S. (1974). Relaxation training for children. *Elementary School Guidance & Counseling, 9*, 14-21. We thank the author for originating the developmentally- appropriate approach to relaxation training with children.

SHOULDERS AND NECK: "Now pretend you are a turtle. You're sitting on a rock by a lake or a peaceful pond just relaxing in the warm sun. It feels nice and warm and safe here. Oh-oh! You sense danger. Pull your head into your house. Try to pull your shoulders up to your ears and push your head down into your shoulders. Hold in tight. It isn't easy to be a turtle in a shell. The danger is past now. You can come out into the warm sunshine and once again you can relax and feel the warm sunshine.

Watch out now! More danger. Hurry, pull your head back into your house and hold it tight. You have to be closed in tight to protect yourself. Okay, you can relax now. Bring your head out and let your shoulders relax. Notice how much better it feels to be relaxed than to be all tight. One more time now! Danger! Pull your head in. Push your shoulders way up to your ears and hold tight. Don't let even a tiny piece of your head show outside your shell. Hold it. Feel the tenseness in your neck and shoulders. Okay. You can come out now. It's safe again. Relax and feel comfortable in your safe place. There's now more danger. Nothing to worry about. Nothing to be afraid of. You feel good. "

JAW: "You have a giant jawbreaker bubble gum in your mouth. It's very hard to chew. Bite down on it. Hard! Let your neck muscles help you. Now relax. Just let your jaw hang loose. Notice how good it feels just to let your jaw drop. Okay, let's tackle that jawbreaker again now. Bite down. Hard! Try to squeeze it out between your teeth. That's good. You're really tearing that gum up. Now relax again. Just let your jaw drop off your face. It feels so good just to let go and not have to fight that bubble gum. Okay, one more time. We're really going to tear it up this time. Bite down. Hard as you can. Harder. Oh, you're really working hard. Good. Now relax. Try to relax your whole body. You've beaten the bubble gum. Let yourself go as loose as you can."

STOMACH: "This time imagine that you want to squeeze through a narrow fence and the boards have splinters on them. You'll have to make yourself very skinny if you're going to make it through. Suck your stomach in. Try to squeeze it up against your backbone. Try to be as skinny as you can. You've got to get through. Now relax. You don't have to be skinny now. Just relax and feel your stomach being warm and loose. Okay, let's try to get through that fence now. Squeeze up your stomach. Make it touch your backbone. Get it real small and tight. Get as skinny as you can. Hold tight, now. You've got to squeeze through. You got through that skinny little fence and no splinters. You can relax now. Settle back and let your stomach come back out where it belongs. You can feel really good now. You've done fine."

LEGS AND FEET: "Now pretend that you are standing barefoot in a big, fat mud puddle. Squish your toes down deep into the mud. Try to get your feet down to the bottom of the mud puddle. You'll probably need your legs to help you push. Push down, spread your toes apart, and feel the mud squish up between your toes. Now step out of the mud puddle. Relax your feet. Let your toes go loose and feel how nice that is. It feels good to be relaxed. Back into the mud puddle.

Squish your toes down. Let your leg muscles help push your feet down. Push your feet. Hard. Try to squeeze that mud puddle dry. Okay. Come back out now. Relax your feet, relax your legs, relax your toes. It feels so good to be relaxed. No tenseness anywhere. You feel kind of warm and tingly."

CONCLUSION: "Stay as relaxed as you can. Let your whole body go limp and feel all your muscles relaxed. In a few minutes I will ask you to open your eyes, and that will be the end of this session. As you go through the day, remember how good it feels to be relaxed. Sometimes you have to make yourself tighter before you can be relaxed, just as we did in these exercises. Practice these exercises every day to get more and more relaxed. A good time to practice is at night, after you have gone to bed and the lights are out and you won't be disturbed. It will help you get to sleep. Then, when you are a really good relaxer, you can help yourself relax here at school. Just remember the turtle, or the jawbreaker, or the mud puddle, and you can do these exercises and nobody will know. You've worked hard today, and it feels good to work hard. Very slowly, now, open your eyes and wiggle your muscles around a little. Very good. You've done a good job. You're going to be a super relaxer."

VIII. The first parent meeting

- This session is devoted to you, the parent(s). As a parent you know your child well. You know what makes your child nervous and what calms him down. You see how anxiety affects your child at home and at school. You know what your child's anxiety does to him both physically and emotionally. Most of all you know how much your child is suffering and the impact that your child's anxiety has not only on him but also on your whole family.

- In this session you have an opportunity to talk with your child's therapist about specific concerns you have. You can help inform your child's therapist about what your child's anxiety looks like at home and how you react to it. What do you do when your child tells you he has a stomachache and can't go to school? How do you react when your child comes to you with a million questions about the thunderstorm that is approaching? What do you do when your child calls you multiple times a day to check in and make sure you are ok?

- It is normal as a parent to want to protect your child. In fact, this is evolutionarily adaptive. Protection becomes a problem however when, as in over-protection, it leads to avoidance. Some parents will do whatever they can to prevent their child from feeling distress.

- What happens when this distress leads you to allow your child to stay home from school? Or leads you to order food for your 13-year-old at a restaurant? By protecting your child from anticipated distress you are also reinforcing their avoidance. While this approach provides relief for your child in the short term, it actually maintains their avoidance in the long term.

- Let's say that your child has a fear of gym class. You let your child go to school late on gym days so that he won't be distressed. While your child's distress decreases when you tell him he can go to school late, you are actually helping increase his fear and distress associated with gym class. You receive a note from school that your child will fail gym if he does not

go. Let's say you decide to have him go to gym class after a month of allowing him to miss it. Your child is now panicked because he hasn't been to gym in a month, he's worried all the kids will make fun of him, and he doesn't know what to do in gym. Because your child had been able to avoid his feared situation (gym), his anxiety/fear of it has actually increased.

- Let's say that instead of letting him avoid gym class you and your child talk to the gym teacher to let him know your child is nervous about gym. You all make an agreement that your child can sit and watch the activity until he feels ready to participate. You find out that your child is nervous because he doesn't know how to play basketball and that is the activity in gym. You decide to help your child face his fear by playing some basketball with him on the weekends. You talk to him about playing at gym on Monday, noting that he will probably feel very nervous at first but the more he plays the more comfortable he will feel. That Monday your child begs you to let him miss gym class, but this time instead of letting him avoid you help him get to gym. As a parent you may experience distress seeing your child upset, but the best thing you can do is help him face his fear.

- During this session your child's therapist will go over specific ways that you can help your child and help yourself.

IX. *The role of anxious self-talk*

- During this session the "E" step of the FEAR plan is introduced. For this step the child checks if he is "**Expecting bad things to happen?**" Many times we feel worried or upset and we don't know why. By asking "what do I expect to happen" your child can help figure out what he is nervous about. As a parent, it is not your job to interrogate or probe…let the therapist work with your child to help him explore his anxious thoughts. The therapist will introduce the role of personal thoughts and their impact on anxiety. As we learned earlier in the program our thoughts, feelings, and behaviors are all interconnected. Your child and therapist will work together to identify thoughts that might occur with different feelings.

- For example, let's say your child and his friend are walking down the street and pass a dog in your neighbor's yard. Your child, being the dog-lover he is, thinks "Oh look how cute and friendly that dog is…let's go pet it." Your child's friend on the other hand is thinking, "Oh my, that dog looks scary…I hope it doesn't bite me." Your child is most likely feeling happy and excited but we probably can't say the same for his friend. Here we see how thoughts can influence how we feel.

- Let's take another example. Let's say that your child's class is going on a field trip to an ice-skating rink. Your child has only been ice-skating once before and he had a great deal of trouble making his way around the rink. Your child's best friend, however, has been taking ice skating lessons since he was a little kid and he loves to skate. When the teacher announced to the class that they were going to go on this field trip what do you think your child was thinking? How about his best friend? Chances are your child was not looking forward to the field trip but his friend was.

- An important part of the *Coping Cat Program* is learning about what we refer to as "self-talk." Self-talk is something that we all do…it is how we pump ourselves up to give that

presentation at work and it's also how we make ourselves nervous about that presentation at work. It is important to learn to identify the difference between anxious self-talk (e.g., I can't do this, I will make a mistake, I always mess up) and coping self-talk (e.g., What's the worst thing that can happen, it won't be that bad, I've done this before so I can do it again).

- When we have anxious self-talk we often find ourselves stuck thinking in a negative or unhelpful way. We refer to this way of thinking as a thinking trap. Here is a list of common thinking traps that can be associated with anxiety:

  - ❖ *Walking with blinders*: Not thinking about all of the possible good things that could happen, only thinking about the bad ones
  - ❖ *The Repetitor*: If it happened once it's always going to happen that way
  - ❖ *The Catastrophe*: Always thinking the worst possible thing will happen
  - ❖ *The Pessimist*: Expecting things to always turn out badly
  - ❖ *Pick, Pick, Pick*: Picking out the negatives in the situation
  - ❖ *The Avoider*: Avoiding or staying away from things that make you nervous
  - ❖ *Quick and dirty*: Jumping to conclusions before getting all the facts
  - ❖ *The Mind Reader*: Reading minds & believing that someone is thinking bad things
  - ❖ *The Shoulds*: I should always get my homework right. I shouldn't feel nervous
  - ❖ *The Fortune Teller*: Predicting what will happen in the future
  - ❖ *The Perfectionist*: "I have to do it right all the time" "I cannot make mistakes"

- Do any of these traps sound familiar to you? Do you find that you engage in any of them? If you do, you might try to catch yourself, and correct yourself.

- As a parent of an anxious child, you may find that you expect bad things to happen when your child tries something anxiety provoking. You may fall into the "fortune teller" thinking trap where you predict that something bad is going to happen. Sometimes our self-talk reflects the beliefs we have about ourselves, our children, and the world. Children with anxiety tend to feel they can't handle stressful situations, yet as a parent it is important to help your child feel competent. We want your child to feel that he can handle stressful situations. In what ways are you helping your child feel competent? In what ways are you sending the message that your child can or can't do something, and what could you do instead?

X. Attitudes and actions

- At this point in the program your child has learned to identify how his body responds to anxiety (e.g., rapid breathing, sweating, shaking, racing heart) and to recognize expectations he may have about a situation (e.g., I can't do this, everyone is going to laugh).

- In this session the next step in the FEAR plan, the "A" step, is introduced. The "A" step stands for "**Attitudes and Actions I can take to help myself feel better.**" This step introduces your child to how he can modify his reactions so that he can proceed even when feeling anxious. Your child and therapist will work together to modify anxious self-talk into coping self-talk.

- *Coping Thoughts:* To modify anxious self-talk into coping self-talk your child first has to identify what he is expecting to happen. Next he will learn to be a "detective" and gather all the evidence about the likelihood of that happening. For example, let's say your child has to give an oral report in history class. He is extremely nervous and his anxious self-talk is telling him, "You are going to mess up and everyone is going to make fun of you."

- Your child will learn to ask himself a series of questions to "challenge" his anxious self talk. These include:

  1. Do I know for sure this is going to happen?

  2. What else might happen?

  3. What has happened before?

  4. Has this happened to anyone else I know?

  5. How likely is it that what I'm expecting is going to happen?

  6. What's the worst thing that could happen?

  7. What would be so bad about that?

  8. Is worrying about this helping?

- After your child and his therapist work through these questions he may realize that he doesn't know that he will mess up for sure; in fact he could do great! He has given oral reports in other classes and he did just fine. Instead of thinking "I'm going to mess up" (anxious self-talk) he thinks to himself, "I've done this before and I can do it again" (coping self-talk).

- Here are some examples of coping thoughts:
  - ❖ Trying is the most important thing
  - ❖ No one is perfect
  - ❖ Every one makes mistakes
  - ❖ I will try my best
  - ❖ I can do it
  - ❖ I will be proud of myself if I try
  - ❖ Go for it!
  - ❖ I have done it before, I can do it again

- It is also important to recognize that a modest level of anxious self-talk is typical…in fact you may also experience this kind of self-talk. Sometimes this self-talk can be excessive but it can be modified with a coping thought. Anxious self-talk often leads to feelings of anxiety and corresponding behavior (avoidance). It is not always possible to completely eliminate our anxious self-talk, but we can help to manage it so that it does not spiral out of control. As a parent it can be helpful to acknowledge your child's feelings and recognize how

distressing anxious self-talk can be. At the same time it is important to note that these are just thoughts and think about what can help so that the thoughts don't spiral out of control.

XI. Problem Solving

- Next your child and therapist will work on the development of problem-solving strategies that can be used when child find himself stuck in an anxiety provoking situation. It is important to note that problem solving is a process. First, the child identifies what is making him feel anxious. Second, the child speculates what he might do to make the situation less anxiety-provoking. Third, the child identifies a range of possible solutions. Last, the child selects the solution that makes the most sense, and proceeds.

- Let's say that your son has to go to softball practice and he can't find his mitt. It is time to leave and he is very anxious about what will happen if he goes to practice without his mitt. Before he decides not to go you sit down with him and begin problem solving. The first step is to define the problem: he can't find his mitt. Next explore potential solutions to the problem. What could your son do to make this situation less upsetting? Allow him to generate ideas: he could look for his mitt, he could tell his coach he is sick and skip practice, he could yell and scream and cry, he could try and think about something else, he could ask you to go to practice and tell his coach he can't find his mitt, or he could go to practice and ask his coach if he has an extra mitt he could use. Next you can help your son evaluate all of the solutions he has come up with. You can work together to decide what might be the best thing to do in this situation.

- As a parent you have probably tried many times before to help your child change his attitude about something. Sometimes this works well and other times your child might be resistant to your input. The process of problem solving is important—don't get upset by a specific solution. The goal of problem solving is not to debate with your child about what the best thing is to do—rather, the goal is to think about a variety of possible solutions. If you find yourself in a tug-of-war with your child gently drop the rope. Sometimes children are resistant to problem solve with their parents and this is when someone outside (i.e., the therapist) can be very helpful.

XII. Results and Rewards

- The final step of the FEAR plan is the "R" step, which stands for "**Results and Rewards**." Your child has learned how to identify when he is feeling anxious, what he is expecting to happen, and some strategies he can use to help himself cope. Now it's time to practice rating and rewarding himself for all his hard work!

- Rewards are given for effort. Sometimes rewards come from other people (e.g., earning a medal or trophy at a race, getting good remarks from a teacher on a test, or getting a present from a parent) and sometimes we reward ourselves (e.g., talking on the phone with a friend, or watching a favorite show on television). During this session your child and therapist will generate a list of rewards your child can earn for coping with his feared situations. It is important to emphasize that we should always reward ourselves for effort even if things

don't go exactly as planned. People are very good at criticizing themselves and often we don't reward ourselves for our hard work.

- When someone is generally anxious and they have to practice doing something that makes them anxious this can be very difficult. Imagine doing something that you are very afraid to do...wouldn't it help to have a reward planned for yourself for after you faced your fear? Some parents struggle with the idea of rewards, but it is important to note the difference between a bribe and a reward. In this program the idea is not to bribe your child (e.g., if you say hi to someone new you will get a toy) but rather reward your child for effort (e.g., I like how brave you were when you said hello to Sam).

- Let's say your child is nervous about going to a sleepover. In the past he has called you and you have always had to pick him up early. Your child and his therapist have made a FEAR plan for the sleepover and he is feeling excited and ready to go. You drop him off and as the hours go by you are surprised and relieved when you don't receive a phone call. It is almost midnight and the phone rings...it's your son. He called to tell you he misses you and he wants to come home. You make an agreement that you will come pick him up first thing in the morning instead of after lunch like you had planned. You help him review some coping strategies and let him know you love him. When you arrive the next morning your son is happy to see you but he is disappointed that he called you and that he isn't able to stay for lunch. You praise your son for making it through the night and pick something special for the two of you to do. Even though he wasn't able to stay as long as he was hoping because he missed you so much he should be reminded and rewarded for how great he did making it through the night.

- In the *Coping Cat Program* we emphasize rewards for effort and for partial success. The important message is that your child tries new and challenging things and is able to cope with the challenges. As your child progresses through the program, and through life, he is likely to find successes and things that could have been done better.

- All of us should reward ourselves for effort and progress, and not just at the times when something goes very well. We focus on the idea that no one does everything perfectly and not doing something 100% correctly does not mean that you punish yourself. Let's look at the famous basketball player Michael Jordan. He is considered to be the greatest player and his shooting average was about 49%...that means that half the time he doesn't make a basket when he shoots.

- As a parent you can sit down with your child and make a list of rewards. Rewards motivate people. Rewards can be both tangible and intangible and they do not need to be big and flashy. As a parent you may not be accustomed to rewarding your child but this is an important part of the program. Eventually the rewards your child has a chance to earn will be the result of his engaging in challenging situations. For example, let's say your child has a fear of speaking to new people. His challenge might be to order ice cream for himself at an unfamiliar store and his reward would be the ice cream. Attention and praise are also very positive rewards. Telling your child "good job" or "nice work" after a challenge is typically rewarding.

- Here are a list of some rewards we have used in our program:

  ❖ Small toy, candy, or treat

  ❖ Playing a game

  ❖ Special time with mom and dad

  ❖ Going to bed 30 minutes past the normal bedtime

  ❖ Selecting what will be served for dinner that night

  ❖ Reading a book with mom or dad

  ❖ Choosing the movie that the family is going to see that weekend

  ❖ Inviting a friend over

  ❖ Praise-- "way to go, nice work, good job"

  ❖ Giving a "high 5"

- At about the middle of the program your child has completed the skills building portion. Now it's time to put the skills to work! Your child and therapist will practice using the FEAR steps in real situations where your child will be anxious or worried. Throughout the skills portion of the program your child and therapist have been working to build a pyramid with a range of situations that make your child nervous. You will find a sample pyramid on page 22.

- During the practice portion of the program your child will work his way up the pyramid. The practice in this program happens gradually, starting with a situation that makes the child a little nervous (e.g., saying hi to a new person) and building up to a situation that makes him very nervous (e.g., reading out loud in class). It is important that you and your child know that the goal of treatment is *not* to remove all of your child's anxiety but to help your child identify and cope with the anxiety.

XIII. The Second Parent Meeting

- Before your child embarks on the practice portion of the program you will have another opportunity to meet with your child's therapist. During this session the therapist will review what your child has learned so far, go over the practice part of the program, and discuss what you can do to continue to facilitate your child's learning. This is a great opportunity to collaborate with your child's therapist about anxiety-provoking situations that you feel would be important for your child to practice. Depending on your child's needs, you may be asked to do some things differently, and to practice doing things differently with the therapist before interacting with your child.

- By this meeting your child has completed the first half of the *Coping Cat Program*, the educational and skill-building portion. He has learned how to:

- ❖ Identify physical feelings of anxiety

- ❖ Connect feelings with thoughts

- ❖ Talk about anxious thoughts and feelings

- ❖ Use relaxation techniques when feeling stressed.

- ❖ Identify when he falls into THINKING TRAPS

- ❖ Come up with COPING THOUGHTS to challenge anxious thoughts

- ❖ Use Problem solving steps

- ❖ Reward himself for TRYING

- Below is the FEAR plan that your child has learned.

  F eeling nervous or scared?

  E xpecting bad things to happen?

  A ttitudes and actions that can help

  R esults and Rewards

- During the next phase of the program, your child will face challenging situations and be rewarded for courageous behavior. Your child will use the FEAR plan in these situations. Practicing the FEAR plan in situations that provoke anxiety allows your child to see that he can cope with the situation.

- It is important to know that your child will experience anxiety when facing challenging situations. This anxiety is to be expected and it is OK. In fact, experiencing anxiety during these tasks is beneficial--it allows your child to apply his newly learned skills set and experience success. The more your child practices using the FEAR plan during anxiety provoking situations the less anxious he will feel and the more his sense of mastery and confidence will build. The FEAR steps need to be practiced repeatedly. Your child will practice being in situations that make him nervous. Practice may continue until your child feels bored with the situation rather than anxious. This practice is done both in and out of the treatment room and the treatment session.

- Your child will stay in the anxiety-provoking situation for a certain duration of time. The aim of the practice tasks (i.e., exposure tasks) is for your child to realize that he can cope with the situation. If your child gets out of the anxiety provoking situation too quickly then he hasn't experienced that he can cope with it and the next time he enters the situation he will likely feel the same or even more anxiety. This is why it is so important to allow your child to stay in the anxiety-provoking situation.

- To help your child in his tasks:

  ❖ Allow your child to trying new things." Encourage courageous behavior.

  ❖ Model courageous behavior by effectively coping with situations that might make YOU nervous.

  ❖ PRAISE, PRAISE, PRAISE

  ❖ Reward brave behavior & trying new things.

  ❖ Permit your child to try things on his own without your help.

  ❖ When your child comes to you with anxious situations, ask him to go over the FEAR plan with you.

  ❖ If your child seems tense or jittery, this may be a time to do some relaxation exercises. Remember that relaxation will only be helpful if this is something that your child has been practicing. You can suggest that your child take some deep breaths or engage in other relaxation techniques but do not push or require anything.

  ❖ When your child makes unrealistic statements, ask your child if he thinks he's falling into a thinking trap. See if your child can describe some coping thoughts. We often want to tell our children, "It will be fine…don't worry." You may have found that this technique does not work very well. It is important to validate your child's feelings and see if he can come up with ways to help himself cope.

  ❖ Encourage problem solving: help your child think of as many solutions to the problem as possible.

  ❖ Help your child APPROACH rather than AVOID challenging situations.

XIV. Facing Fears

- During the remainder of the program your child will be practicing his newly learned skills by doing practices. These practices will take place during session and throughout the week. You, your child, and his therapist will work to think of situations that are anxiety-provoking for your child. These situations will be placed on a FEAR Pyramid with the least anxiety-provoking situations at the bottom and the most anxiety-provoking situations at the top

- Throughout the program your child will work his way to the top of his FEAR Pyramid. On the next page you will find a sample of a FEAR Pyramid for a child who is worried about social evaluation and has great difficulty talking to people. Notice that the items on the lower portion of the pyramid are easier than the items towards the top.

- It is important to know that some children get very anxious before facing their feared situations. Some children also become angry when they are anxious. As a parent you may need extra help and support for yourself. You can ask your child's therapist for recommendations about how to support yourself during this process.

- You may be asked to participate in the practices (i.e., exposure tasks) in a variety of ways. Sometimes your job may be to take a step back and have your child practice doing something you normally do for him. For example, let's say that when you go out to eat you always order food for your son. One of his challenges may be to order for himself at a restaurant. Your involvement in his challenge will be NOT to order for him. This may be very difficult for you and for your child. You do not want to see him distressed but you know how important it is that he orders for himself. What can you do to help yourself through this situation so you don't jump in and "rescue" your child by ordering for him? Ideas for helping you cope can be strategized with the therapist.

Sample Fear Pyramid

Wow, this makes me feel really, really scared

→ Read out loud in class

This makes me feel really scared

→ Read out loud to a group of people at the clinic

This makes me feel scared

→ Call a friend on the phone

This makes me feel a little scared

→ Play a game with a new person at the clinic

→ Say "hi" to a new person

This makes me feel uncomfortable

→ Wave to a new person at school

- Your involvement in your child's exposure tasks may also involve planning things in advance. Let's say that your child is afraid of being away from you. One of his challenges may be to go to his friend's house while you run some errands. Your son has a play date this coming Saturday. When you drop him off at his friend's you notice that you are feeling nervous. What if he cries and begs you not to go? It can be normal for a parent to be nervous when your child is trying something new. What are some strategies you can use to help yourself feel less nervous? Remember to model being brave.

- Each week your child comes to session he will be engaging in more and more challenging tasks. It is important to praise your child for his efforts.

- As your child is learning to manage his anxiety it is also likely that changes are occurring in family relationships. What is different now that your child is becoming more independent and/or less anxious? What is changing now that you are accommodating your child's anxiety less? Have you noticed any other changes

XV. Time to Celebrate

- After all of the challenging tasks, the final session is a time to celebrate your child's hard work and success. Most children benefit from our program. Some children make more gains than others. It is important to solidify the gains that your child has made.

- One way we do this is in the form of a pizza party which usually takes place during the last session of treatment. Your child can invite whomever he wants to attend. Also, your child and therapist will work together to help your child produce a "commercial" about all that he has learned and done in the program. This provides your child with an opportunity to show off his newly acquired skills.

- Your child can teach the FEAR plan to everyone in the room. He might choose to do this in the form of a song or poem or he might have a collage with pictures of all the brave things he's done. Your child will receive a certificate of completion from the therapist that he can take home and hang on the wall. Today is the day that your child "graduates" from the program. This does not mean that all of your child's anxiety is gone. Rather, it is the time to focus on all the gains your child has made but also recognize that there are still challenges in the future.

XVI. The End of Treatment

- The end of treatment is both an exciting and potentially anxiety provoking time. You and your child have worked very hard and seen some gains. However, there will be additional challenges that your child will have to face. Throughout the program your child has gathered a set of tools (e.g., relaxation techniques, coping thoughts) to cope with anxiety. These are tools that he can carry with him and use in a variety of situations…not just the ones he practiced during the program. Throughout life your child will encounter a number of stressful situations and you can't protect him from all of them. The goal of the *Coping Cat Program* is

to teach your child skills that he can use throughout his life. Although the nature of the anxiety-provoking situation may change (e.g., being nervous about going on a sleepover, worrying about the first day of high school) the basics (e.g. somatic reactions, anxious-self talk) will likely be the same.

- As the parent you have learned some ways to help your child cope with anxiety. But what happens if your child starts to become anxious again? First, it is important to remember that it is not uncommon for children to have setbacks. But, a "lapse" is not a "collapse." Our experience is that children who have completed the program recover more quickly from these setbacks than they did before the program. Setbacks can be small (e.g., your child slept in your bed for one night) or they can become bigger (e.g., your child has slept in your bed several nights this week). If the setback becomes troubling, it might be a good time to review the *Coping Cat workbook* and put in place some strategies. For some children, having a booster session with the therapist can be very helpful.

- You can also help your child by reviewing the F.E.A.R. plan with him. On the next page you will find a review of what your child has learned throughout the program.

The FEAR Plan- A Coping Guide

1) **F-** Am I feeling anxious or frightened?
   - Pay attention to my body-- stomach aches, headaches, heart pounding, feeling warm, restless, irritable-- these can all be signs of anxiety
   - Start off by doing some deep breathing- maybe even other relaxation strategies. Relax.
   - Now it is time to put the rest of the FEAR plan into action

2) **E-** What am I expecting will happen? What is my self-talk?
   - Pay attention to my thoughts-- what am I thinking, what am I asking myself?
   - Does it sound like I am falling into a thinking trap?
   - Watch out for these thinking traps
     - *Walking with blinders:* Not thinking about all of the possible good things that could happen, only thinking about the bad ones
     - *The Repetitor:* If it happened once it's always going to happen that way
     - *The Catastrophe:* Always thinking the worst possible thing will happen
     - *The Pessimist:* Expecting things to always turn out badly
     - *Pick, Pick, Pick:* Picking out the negatives in the situation
     - *The Avoider:* Avoiding or staying away from things that make you nervous
     - *The Mind Reader:* reading minds & believing that someone is thinking bad things
     - *The Shoulds:* I should always get my homework right. I shouldn't feel nervous
     - *The Fortune Teller:* Predicting what will happen in the future
     - *The Perfectionist:* "I have to do it right all the time" "I cannot make mistakes"

3) **A-** What are attitudes and actions that might help? What is a coping thought that I could have in this situation?
   - Gather evidence for the thought. Do I know for sure this is going to happen?
   - What else might happen in this situation?
   - How many times has this happened before? How likely is it this will happen?
   - What is the worst thing that could happen? What would be so bad about that?
   - Begin *problem solving!*

4) **R-** Results and rewards- yeah! You did it!
   - See that wasn't so bad. Next time you'll be able to do it with no problem
   - Give yourself rewards for all of your accomplishments, not just when you do something perfectly

XVII. Books and Resources

Some parents also find it helpful to read additional materials. Below is a list of useful resources for parents, teachers, and children about anxiety and its treatment.

Books about Anxiety for Parents & Teachers

Chansky, T. E. (2004). *Freeing your child from anxiety: Powerful, practical solutions to overcome your child's fears, worries, and phobias.* New York , NY , USA: Broadway Books.

Manassis, K. (1996). *Keys to parenting an anxious child.* Hauppauge, New York , USA: Baron's Educational Series, Inc.

Rapee, R. M., Spence, S. H., Cobham, V., & Wignall, A. M. (2000). *Helping your anxious child: A step-by-step guide for parents.* Oakland, CA: New Harbinger Publications Inc.

Books about Anxiety for Children

Henkes, K. (2000). *Wemberly worried.* Hong Kong, South China: Greenwillow Books, Harper Collins Publishers.

Huebner, D. (2005). *What to Do When You Worry Too Much: A Kid's Guide to Overcoming Anxiety.* Washington, DC: Magination Press.

Tompkins, M.A., and Martinez, K.A. (2009). *My Anxious Mind: A Teen's Guide to Managing Anxiety and Panic.* Washington, DC: Magination Press.

Coping Cat Program Resources

Kendall, P.C., & Hedtke, K.A. (2006). *Cognitive-Behavioral Therapy for Anxious Children: Therapist Manual, 3rd Edition.* Ardmore, PA: Workbook Publishing.

Kendall, P.C., & Hedtke, K.A. (2006). *Coping Cat Workbook, 2nd Edition.* Ardmore, PA: Workbook Publishing. www.workbookpublishing.com

Internet Resources

The Child Anxiety Network: www.childanxiety.net

Association for Behavioral & Cognitive Therapies: www.abct.org

Anxiety Disorders Association of America: www.adaa.org

The Center for Mental Health Services: www.mentalhealth.org

Child and Adolescent Anxiety Disorders Clinic at Temple University www.childanxiety.org

ISBN: 978-1-888805-43-7